Artists' Workshop

Portraits

Penny King and Clare Roundhill

 Crabtree Publishing Company

Artists' Workshop

Crabtree Publishing Company

350 Fifth Avenue
Suite 3308
New York, NY 10118

360 York Road, R.R.4
Niagara-on-the-Lake
Ontario L0S 1J0

73 Lime Walk
Headington, Oxford
England 0X3 7AD

Edited by **Bobbie Kalman**
Designed by **Jane Warring**
Illustrations by **Lindy Norton**
Children's pictures and sculptures by
**Amber Civardi, Davina Clarke, Camilla Cramsie, Charlotte Downham,
Ellie Grace, Lara Haworth, Lucinda Howells, Sophie Johns, Abby Kirvan,
Rosanna Kirvan, Freddie Marriage, Gussie Pownall, Leo Thomson
Lucy Stratton, Isabella Milne, Victoria Arbuthnot, Leonora Bowen**
Photographs by **Peter Millard**

Created by
Thumbprint Books

Copyright © 1996 Thumbprint Books

Cataloging-in-publication data
King, Penny. 1963-
Portraits/Penny King & Clare Roundhill.
p. cm. -- (Artists' workshop)
Includes index.
Summary: Presents six portraits to be used as starting points for exploring various
artistic techniques. Includes instructions and examples for creating one's own work.
ISBN 0-86505-850-4 (hc). -- ISBN 0-86505-860-1 (paper)
1. Art--Technique--Juvenile literature. 2. Portraits -- Juvenile literature.
[1. Art -- Technique. 2. Portraits.]
I. Roundhill, Clare, 1964- . II. Title. III. Series
N7575.K52 1996   704.9'42--dc20   95-50853
CIP
AC

First published 1996 by
A & C Black Publishers Ltd
37 Soho Square, London, W1D 3QZ
www.acblack.com

Printed and bound in Singapore

Cover Photograph: **Vincent Van Gogh** Postman Roulin.
When Van Gogh lived in the South of France, he became
friends with this postman, who brought him letters from
his brother Theo. Van Gogh painted several portraits of him.

Contents

Looking at portraits

'Every time I paint a portrait, I lose a friend'. A famous American artist called John Singer Sargent once made this statement because his friends thought he painted them a little too realistically!

Before photography was invented, important people such as kings, queens or rich merchants paid artists to paint their portraits.

These portraits not only showed what people looked like, they were also full of clues about their lives. Rulers were often shown with their crowns and robes. Rich people were shown wearing expensive clothes and jewels. Soldiers wore their uniforms and carried weapons.

The invention of photography gave people an easier way to make realistic portraits. Artists thought there was no point in copying photography and started thinking of new ways to create portraits. They often used color in different and unusual ways to express a person's feelings and moods.

François-Hubert Drouais (1727-1775)
Madame de Pompadour Musée Condé, Chantilly

Portraits can be created in many ways—as paintings, drawings, photographs or sculptures. This book contains six portraits—two very old and the rest more modern. Each of them has been created using a different technique.

You can learn what gave the artists the ideas for creating these portraits and discover how they made them. Borrow their ideas, add your own, and create new portraits. The pictures drawn by children will help you.

You can create a portrait any way you choose. Either make it look as much as possible like the person you are painting or give an impression of the person's mood. You can show a front or side view (known as a profile).

Your portrait might be in full color or in black and white. You can make your subject look pretty or ugly and frightening. You can also paint a portrait of yourself. This is called a self-portrait. The choice is yours!

Egyptian effects

Would you believe that this picture is over 3,000 years old? It was painted on the floor of the tomb of an Ancient Egyptian official. It is a portrait of a king called Amenophis I and is surrounded by symbols—pictures with special meanings.

Dead King Amenophis I © British Museum

The Egyptians believed that when people died, they went to a new world with their belongings. They looked forward to their new life and were not frightened of dying.

Their bodies were dried out and wrapped in linen bandages. These preserved bodies were called mummies. The mummies were put in coffins inside painted tombs.

Every picture around the portrait of Amenophis I has an important meaning.

▶ The sun is shown as a red disc moving across the sky on wings. It is protected by two serpents.

◀ The cobra on the king's forehead is a symbol of the sun. It spits fire to protect the king from his enemies.

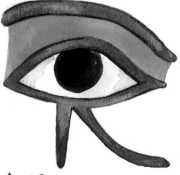

crook

flail

▶ The feather pattern on the king's clothes shows that he was mummified. The pattern represents the wings of the goddesses wrapped around his body to protect him.

▲ Kings are often shown carrying a crook and a flail in their hands. These are symbols of kingship.

◀ The ankh is a symbol of everlasting life. Only kings and queens were allowed to carry one, since only they had the power to give or take a life.

▼ The vulture represents Upper Egypt, which was once ruled by this king.

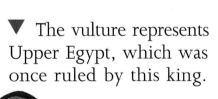

▲ The eye represents the eye of Horus. It was damaged during a fight for the throne of Egypt and restored by magic. It shows that everything is still perfect and healthy, even after death.

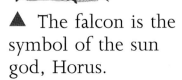

▲ The falcon is the symbol of the sun god, Horus.

An imaginary journey

Imagine you or a friend are moving to a new world. Decide what you would take with you on your journey and then paint a portrait surrounded by these important possessions.

Perhaps you would take a favorite pet, toy, book, hat, or the food you like best. Paint pictures that show your interests, just as the Egyptians did.

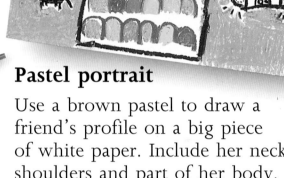

Pastel portrait

Use a brown pastel to draw a friend's profile on a big piece of white paper. Include her neck, shoulders and part of her body. Look at the colors on the Egyptian tomb painting. Choose similar colors for your portrait.

You can mix pastels together to make different colors. Press hard and use lots of strokes to get a dark color. Rub it gently into the paper with your fingertips or a cotton ball.

Draw a pattern all over the clothes and color it in with pastels. Make the background a pale, sandy color. Draw pictures of your friend's favorite things all over it.

Egyptian mummy portrait

Ask your mother to sit sideways between a lamp and some paper stuck to the wall behind her. Draw carefully around her shadow.

Paint features on the face with watercolors or poster paint, trying to match skin, hair and eye colors. To create an Egyptian look, outline the eyes and whole portrait in black.

When your picture is dry, cut it out and glue it to a big piece of brightly colored paper. Ask your mother what things she would take with her to a new world and then paint them on the background paper.

If you need to add any details, let the bottom colors dry first, otherwise the paints might run into one another. Give each picture a dark outline.

Your favorite things

Put on the things you would like to wear on an imaginary journey to a new world—perhaps a favorite hat or cap. Look at yourself in the mirror and paint your portrait on a sheet of brightly colored paper. Outline all the features with black paint.

Choose ten important items you would take with you. Cut out pictures of these items from magazines, and glue them around your portrait.

Magnificent mosaics

This picture is called a mosaic. Mosaics are made with lots of small pieces of a hard material, such as stone, tile or glass. The pieces are glued or cemented close together on a flat surface.

Head of Neptune, Roman Ancient Art & Architecture Collection, London

This mosaic shows the head of Neptune, the Roman god of the sea. The Romans believed he lived in an underwater palace with his wife.

He is always shown as an old man with long wavy hair and a long spiky beard. Sometimes he holds a three-pronged spear called a trident.

▶ Long ago, the Greeks and Romans used mosaics to decorate their floors and walls. These pictures told stories of people, animals or battles.

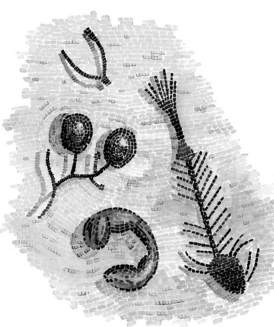

◀ Sometimes, as a joke, the mosaic makers put in pictures of fish bones and other scraps of food, so that it looked as if people had dropped them on the floor.

▼ Look how the main shapes of the mosaic have a dark outline. Mosaics are meant to be seen at a distance. The outlines help them stand out.

▲ Other people, called Byzantines, made magnificent glass and gold mosaics of emperors and saints dressed in rich-looking costumes.

Making a mosaic picture

Using pieces cut from magazines or wrapping paper, make your own mosaics. You might prefer to draw a mosaic picture instead.

Magazine mosaic

Before you begin your mosaic picture, make a colored sketch of it first.

Look through old magazines for the colors you need. Choose colors that match the sketch you have drawn.

Cut out big squares for the background and small squares for the details of the face and clothes. You may need more of some colors than others.

Cut lots of shades of the same color—some dark, some light. Keep each shade in a separate pile.

Glue the squares on another piece of paper, matching the colors of your sketch. It takes a long time, but it's worth it!

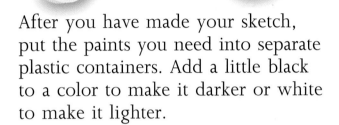

Printed mosaic

Cut an old sponge into big and small cubes.

After you have made your sketch, put the paints you need into separate plastic containers. Add a little black to a color to make it darker or white to make it lighter.

Before you start your real picture, practice printing on newspaper first. Use one sponge cube for each shade. Print the eyes, nose and mouth first. Then fill in the rest of the face.

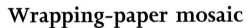

Wrapping-paper mosaic

Cut colored paper, wrapping paper, or old birthday and Christmas cards into squares. Use them to create different textures and patterns in your picture.

13

Swirls of color

Vincent Van Gogh, a Dutch artist, painted this portrait of himself a few months before he died. He was one of the first painters to use colors to show moods and feelings, instead of trying to paint in realistic colors. How do you think he was feeling when he painted this picture?

Vincent Van Gogh Self-Portrait 1889. Musée d'Orsay, Paris

Van Gogh painted very quickly. He used thick, bold strokes that swirl, curl and spiral. Sometimes he was in such a hurry that he squeezed paint straight onto a canvas and spread it with his fingers.

Color was very important to Van Gogh. His early pictures of Dutch peasants were dark and sad, to show the hard lives these people led.

Later, he moved to the South of France and started painting with purer, brighter colors, which showed the shimmering heat and light of his surroundings. Van Gogh loved nature and liked painting outdoors. His pictures of flowers and trees are full of joy and yellow sunshine.

Van Gogh himself, however, was often unhappy. Once, when he was very miserable, he cut off part of his ear. After that, he painted several self-portraits, which showed his loneliness. The pale, icy colors of his self-portrait, opposite, emphasise his unhappy feelings.

Painting a self-portrait

Use the same rich style as Van Gogh to paint a self-portrait that shows how you feel as well as how you look. The best way to get a good likeness of yourself is to copy a photograph or look at your face in the mirror as you draw. Mix poster paint with flour and glue to make it thick and shiny.

Drawing faces

Draw an oval face. Lightly sketch a line across it, halfway down, marking the position for your eyes and the tops of your ears. Draw another line halfway between this line and the chin. The tip of your nose will rest here. Divide the bottom section in half to find where to draw your mouth.

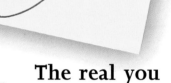

The real you

Do you have a big or small nose, brown or blue eyes, fair or dark hair? Paint a portrait that looks as much like you as possible, mixing colors to match your features. To get rough and smooth textures, spread on swirls, dots, lines and dashes of thick paint with a brush, lollipop stick or your fingertips.

A moody portrait

How are you feeling today—hot with anger, pale with fatigue, or sparkling with excitement? Once you've decided, paint a portrait of yourself using colors that match your mood. Don't worry about making your skin color realistic. Just use the colors that you think show your feelings best.

Background blast

Paint a portrait of yourself, but this time, make a moody background to show how you feel. You might paint swirls of yellow and orange if you are in a happy mood, blue blobs if you are feeling sad, purple and black streaks if you are angry, or sparks and dashes of red if you are excited.

Line and pattern portraits

The famous Spanish artist, Pablo Picasso, created this portrait, using lines and patterns to give it texture and a feeling of depth. He colored only the areas that he thought were the most important.

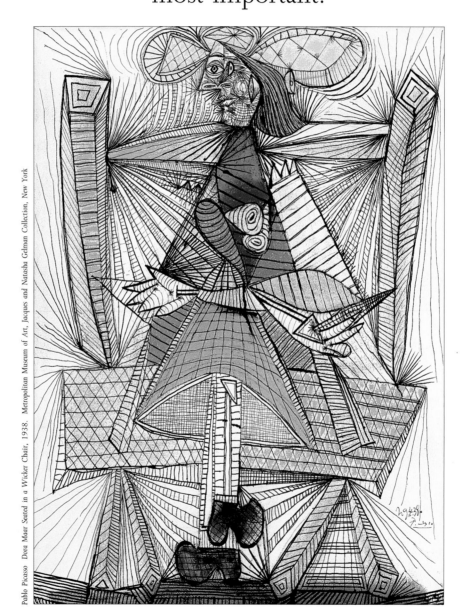

Pablo Picasso Dora Maar Seated in a Wicker Chair, 1938. Metropolitan Museum of Art, Jacques and Natasha Gelman Collection, New York

Picasso met Dora Maar, the woman in the picture, in a café in Paris. He was fascinated by her hands, with their long red fingernails.

He watched Dora play a curious game with a knife. She flicked the blade between her fingers, sometimes cutting herself.

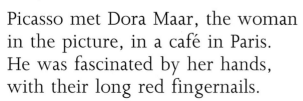

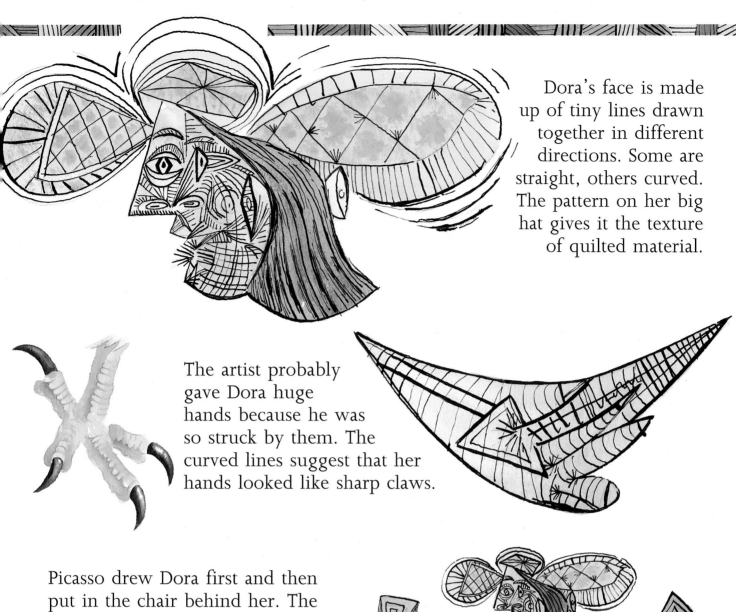

Dora's face is made up of tiny lines drawn together in different directions. Some are straight, others curved. The pattern on her big hat gives it the texture of quilted material.

The artist probably gave Dora huge hands because he was so struck by them. The curved lines suggest that her hands looked like sharp claws.

Picasso drew Dora first and then put in the chair behind her. The crisscross pattern on the seat makes it look as if it is made of wicker. The lines on the back and legs of the chair resemble woodgrain.

To give a feeling of depth, Picasso drew a background of lines traveling in all directions. Perhaps he was trying to make it look as if a spider was spinning its web around Dora, protecting her and trapping her at the same time.

Dora looks a little like a doll sitting in a toy chair, her eyes staring and arms loosely folded. There is something about her that doesn't seem quite real.

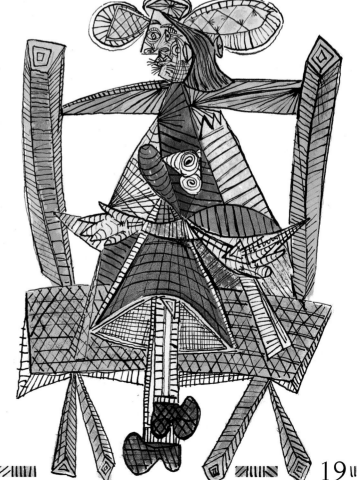

Line design

Try drawing your own line and pattern portraits. The lines can be thick or thin, curved or wavy, close or far apart, straight or crooked, zigzagged or crisscrossed. Use the lines to create different textures, such as a wool sweater, a cotton dress, thick hair or wrinkled skin.

Simple sketch

The easiest way to draw someone sitting in a chair is to draw the person first and then put in the chair behind her.

Funny face

Draw the outline of a friend's head in profile. Decide which is her strongest feature. If it is her nose, then draw it a bit bigger than you normally would.

Draw in the hair, eyes, ears and mouth. They don't have to be true to life. Look at how Picasso has mixed up Dora's features and given her bell-shaped ears, big flaring nostrils and strange-looking eyes.

Fill in the face with tiny lines, either straight or curved. Use crayons or felt-tipped pens to color the parts you think are important.

Lots of lines

Draw a portrait of a friend sitting in a chair, making it look as much like Picasso's picture as you can.

Fill in the face, hair, clothes, shoes and chair with different kinds of lines and patterns. Use the lines to give your picture texture and a feeling of depth. Paint the most important parts.

Crisscrossed wax portrait

This time, draw the outline of your portrait using a felt-tipped pen. Fill it in with lines and patterns, using a colored wax crayon. Add a web of lines in the background.

Use different colored felt-tipped pens to color over the most important areas of your picture. The wax lines will resist the felt-tipped pens to give an unusual effect.

Skinny sculptures

A Swiss artist, called Alberto Giacometti, made this sculpture out of bronze. He called it Man Pointing. Giacometti is well known for his long, thin sculptures of people. As he worked at his sculptures, they became thinner and thinner.

Alberto Giacometti Man Pointing, 1947 Tate Gallery, London

Giacometti was influenced by a group of artists called Surrealists. They preferred to paint pictures from their imagination, from memory or from dreams rather than from real life.

This sketch and the painting below were inspired, but not drawn, by Giacometti.

The people in Giacometti's sculptures and paintings often look sad and lonely. He thought they looked more lifelike if they were very small or very thin.

Giacometti used earthy colors in his paintings and sculptures. His favorite color was gray. Although people told him to use bright colors, he paid no attention.

Wiry walkers

Create your own Giacometti-style sculptures using wire, tin foil, clay or papier mâché. Ask friends to pose for you outdoors in the afternoon sun. Look at and sketch the long, thin shadows made by their bodies. Draw several poses to give you different ideas for your skinny sculptures.

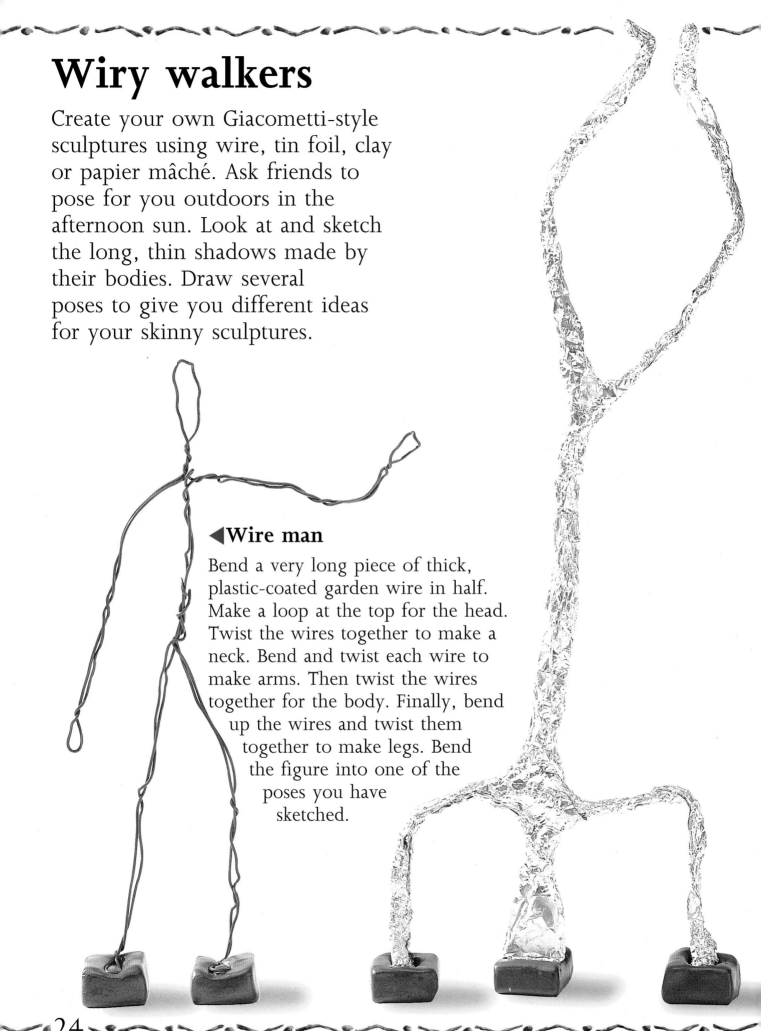

◀Wire man

Bend a very long piece of thick, plastic-coated garden wire in half. Make a loop at the top for the head. Twist the wires together to make a neck. Bend and twist each wire to make arms. Then twist the wires together for the body. Finally, bend up the wires and twist them together to make legs. Bend the figure into one of the poses you have sketched.

◀ Tin-foil figure

Make a wire figure as you did before. Cover it with strips of tin foil, scrunched firmly around the body. To make your sculpture look more colorful, you can add shiny candy wrappers. Press the figure into clay if you want it to stand up.

▼ Clay child

Make a wire figure. Roll balls of self-hardening clay into long, soft, sticky sausage shapes. Pull off small pieces at a time and press them onto the wire frame. If you wish, you can paint colorful decorations all over your clay figure when it has dried.

▲ Papier mâché person

Mix a half cup of flour with enough water to make a thick, smooth paste. Add a tablespoon of glue. Dip strips of colored magazine pages into the mixture. Wrap them around a wire figure. Try not to get too much glue mixture on the paper strips.

Photo portraits

Can you see how this portrait is made from many photographs of the same person, taken from different angles? This technique is called photo-montage. The portrait is by a British artist called David Hockney. It shows his mother.

David Hockney Mother Yorkshire Moors 1982 © D. Hockney 1982

Hockney wanted to show every detail of his mother. He took photos of her from the front and the side.

Then he joined them together in his picture. Some pictures were taken closer up than others. Which ones?

Notice how the photos overlap to bring out particular features, such as hair and wrinkles. They are carefully arranged and pasted down to make a whole portrait. Hockney didn't worry that the edges were ragged.

The first cameras were big and heavy. Only a few people knew how to use them. Photographers had studios where families went to have their pictures taken. They stood or sat in front of a painted cloth background.

The photos were only in black and white and took a long time to take. People had to stand still for several minutes, so their image did not blur. That is why people in old photographs often look so stiff and serious.

Modern cameras are cheaper and easier to use. Anyone can buy a camera and take quick photographs in color. Compare a photo of yourself with one of your grandmother when she was little.

Photo fitting

Create your own montages using photographs, drawings or pictures cut from magazines. They will look even better if you use side views as well as front views.

Spend time laying down the pictures in different positions until you are pleased with the way your montage looks. You can either overlap the pictures or leave gaps to make really interesting shapes.

Photo montage

Ask someone to take lots of photographs of you while you are outside facing the sun. Get the person to take pictures of different features of your face—your forehead, eyes, chin, ears, hair, mouth and nose—both side and front views.

The photographer will move around you, but you must keep very still. Remind him or her to keep the camera as still as possible when shooting.

When the photographs have been developed, choose the ones you like best for your montage. Cut them up if you need to and then lay them out to create an interesting image.

Glue the photographs onto stiff cardboard two at a time, so that you don't disturb the whole picture. Glue the bottom ones first.

Magazine montage

Cut out three different faces, all about the same size, from old magazines. Cut the features from all three faces into squares, strips or rectangles. Mix them up and create a montage, using features from different faces.

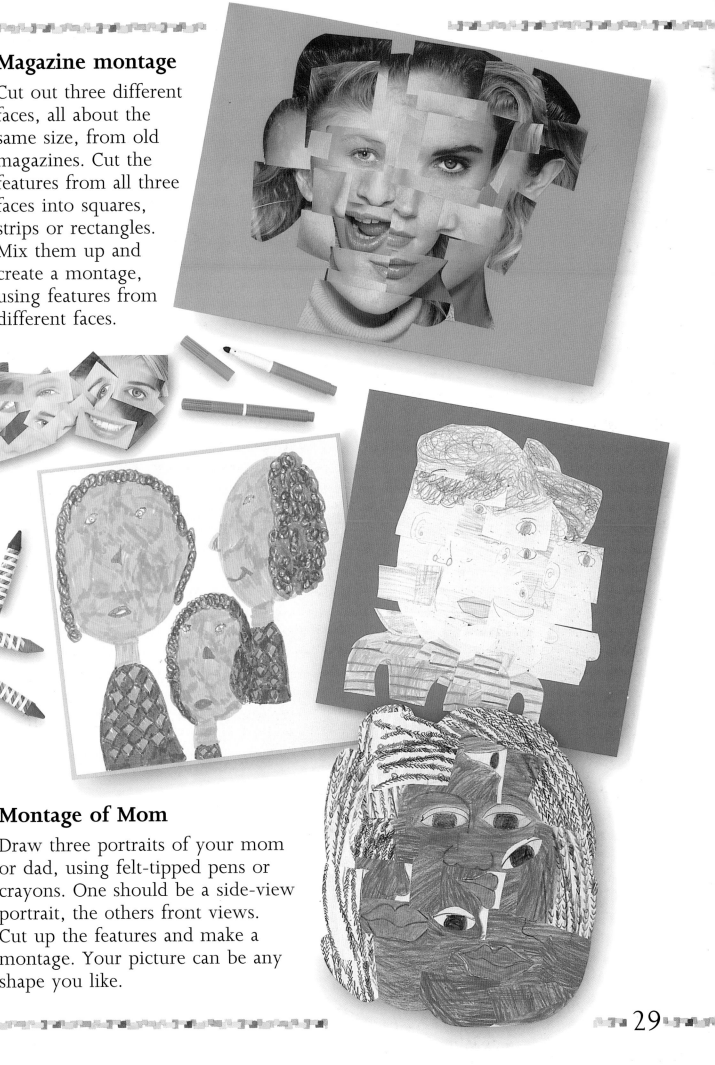

Montage of Mom

Draw three portraits of your mom or dad, using felt-tipped pens or crayons. One should be a side-view portrait, the others front views. Cut up the features and make a montage. Your picture can be any shape you like.

More about the artists

Egyptian painters

Dead King Amenophis I, 1050 BC

Egyptian artists were specially trained to paint spells on coffins and scenes on the walls of tombs of kings and other important people. People believed that the spells would protect the dead and that the scenes would work by magic to give the dead kings everything they needed for living in the next world. The artists ground their own colors from minerals. They used charcoal for black and ochre for red.

Roman mosaic makers

Head of Neptune, c.500AD

Mosaic makers were very skilled. They made their own cubes, called tesserae, from different colored materials, such as sandstone, limestone, marble and brick. First they sawed the hard stone into thin sticks. Then they hammered these sticks over a sharp chisel head to cut them into cubes. Mosaics are very long lasting. Many of them still survive today, hundreds of years after they were first made.

Vincent Van Gogh

(1853- 1890   Dutch)
Self-portrait, 1889

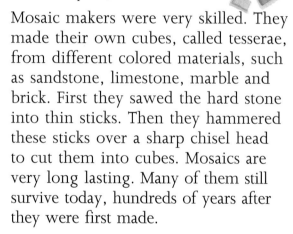

Van Gogh worked as a schoolmaster and missionary before he became a painter. He taught himself to draw and paint with oil paints. He painted everyday scenes such as landscapes, flowers, his bedroom, a chair and portraits of himself and his neighbors in a bold and exciting way. He sold only one painting during his lifetime, but now his paintings sell for millions of dollars. Perhaps his most famous paintings are of sunflowers. Van Gogh signed his paintings with just his first name, Vincent.

Pablo Picasso

(1881 - 1973   Spanish)
Dora Maar seated in a Wicker Chair, 1938

Picasso was one of the most famous and important artists of this century. His father was an artist as well and taught Picasso to draw when he was a young child. Picasso spent his life experimenting with new ways of painting and sculpting. He helped invent a style of art called Cubism, which showed objects, landscapes and people in geometric shapes, often in browns or grays.

Alberto Giacometti

(1901 - 1966   Swiss)
Man Pointing, 1947

By the time Giacometti was a teenager, he was already good at sculpture and painting. Later, he made sculptures of thin human figures, either on their own or in groups. These were usually set upon thick, heavy bases. Giacometti was interested in the shapes a figure made in the space around it and in the relationship between several figures. *Man Pointing* is one of his most famous sculptures. His paintings were almost always of people, painted in shades of brown and gray.

David Hockney

(Born 1937   British)
Mother photo-montage, 1982

David Hockney is a popular modern painter. Many of his paintings show the people he knows or the places where he has lived. He has spent many years in California and has painted different views of it. One of his more famous paintings is *A Bigger Splash* (1967), which shows a Californian swimming pool. He often uses photography and has created many kinds of photo-montages.

Other things to do

3 Find a big sheet of clear plastic and a passport-sized photograph of yourself. Draw a dozen or more outlines of your face on the plastic, using the photo as a guide. Now draw all kinds of hairstyles on the plastic—long, short, curly and even multi-colored. Put your photograph under each style to see which one suits you best!

1 Make a collection of portraits. See how many different types you can find—for example, coins, stamps, photographs, drawings, cartoons and postcards. They will give you ideas for creating portraits of your own.

2 Look at recent photographs of people in your family and at photographs of older members of your family, taken when they were young. What family likenesses can you see? Draw what you think your face will look like in twenty or thirty years' time.

4 Draw a self-portrait or choose a photograph of yourself. Glue it onto a piece of stiff cardboard, large enough to frame the picture. Decorate the frame in an unusual way, either by painting it with patterns or gluing on sequins, lace, wrapping paper, tiny beads or shells.

Index

Acknowledgments
*The publishers are grateful to the following institutions
and individuals for permission to reproduce the
illustrations on the pages mentioned.*
The Museum of Modern Art, New York/Bridgeman
Art Library, London: cover; Musée Condé, Chantilly,
Giraudon/ Bridgeman Art Library, London: 4; © The
British Museum: 6; The Ancient Art and Architecture
Collection: 10; Musée d'Orsay/Visual Arts Library:
14; The Metropolitan Museum of Art, Jacques and
Natasha Gelman collection, New York © DACS 1996:
18; Courtesy of Association Alberto and Annette
Giacometti, Paris. Photo by Sabine Weiss, Paris,
© DACS 1996; Tate Gallery, London: 22; David
Hockney/Tradhart Ltd: 26.

3 4 5 6 7 8 9 0 Printed in Singapore 6 5 4 3 2 1 0